Elevate Empathy

The Power of Kindness

Elevate Empathy

The Power of Kindness

Edited by David Theune
with Carlyn Arteaga

Three Leaf Press

Published by Three Leaf Press
www.threeleafpress.com

ISBN: 978-0692298831

Cover and interior design by Daniel Ireland

Printed in the United States of America
First edition: September 2014

Acknowledgments

No book writes itself and there are some folks that deserve some special attention. Quite frankly, if it weren't for these people, there would be no book.

Emily Bazelon's support of this book and this project has been essential to our moving forward with the publishing. At every turn, she has been outstanding and deserves much credit. Our book publisher, Daniel Ireland of Three Leaf Press, is the one who has made the book look good. He has also agreed to publish under the rarest of terms: not for profit. Daniel is patient and full of helpful thoughts and encouragement. We must acknowledge the efforts of our many proofreaders who gave us thoughts and suggestions throughout the process—specifically, Joe Sinn and Jessie Vought. Most importantly, though, this book could not have happened without the vulnerability and skill of its contributors. They are, all of them, the embodiment of empathy and, above all, they care about the people of the world.

This book, though, is about more than its writing. It's also a suggestion to other communities to try a community book club of their own and there are many people who must be thanked for making the book club itself come to fruition.

Without the good grace of superintendent Dennis Furton and the other school administrators, this book club would never have gotten off the ground. Together, we held many conversations as the book club was just starting and we praise the administrators' willingness to have this sometimes-difficult conversation. The book club committee really made the book club what it was. They were the ones to reach out to others and spread the word. They pounded the pavement. Katie Bator, Jill Garrison, Sarah Lewakowski, Garth Trask, Pete Yoshonis, and Laurie Whitaker brought humans to the idea. The hosts of our EAT WITH EIGHT event were willing to accept others into their home and communicate with book club members so all voices could be heard. Finally, and most importantly, we want to thank the community book club participants. Because of you, the vital topic of empathy came alive. You modeled literacy and kindness for the entire community. We know you will keep that message going through your children, your neighbors—anyone you meet.

—*David Theune & Carlyn Arteaga*

Contents

Introduction

IN THE YEARS THAT I worked on writing my book, *Sticks and Stones: Defeating the Culture of Bullying and Rediscovering the Power of Character and Empathy*, my hope was to find readers like David Theune and the folks of Spring Lake, Michigan. For me, watching a community read my book together, as a springboard for thought and conversation, was all I could ask for. It was both instructive and great fun to read the tweets and Facebook posts that came out of this community book club—to follow along as people absorbed the stories and ideas in my book and applied them to their own lives.

Now I've had the pleasure of reading 20 longer responses that David has collected from the group that read *Sticks and Stones* as a community endeavor. These pieces are full of insight and wisdom, writ small and writ large, and I'm honored to have played a small part in spurring this project.

One of the most important lessons I learned in working on my book is that it doesn't take heroic action to be what educators increasingly call an upstander—a person who sees unkindness or bullying and tries to put a stop to it. Stan Davis and Charisse Nixon surveyed thousands of teenagers who'd been bullied (for their book, *Youth Voice Project*) to find out what they'd found to be the most helpful response from their peers. The teenagers were just as likely to choose a small moment of empathy—a friendly hand on the shoulder, a sympathetic text message, the simple question "are you OK?"—as a big "HEY STOP IT!" response to an aggressor.

I find this insight reassuring and heart warming. It redefines upstanding so that it's about standing with the victim as much or more as standing up to the person who is acting like a bully. (Maybe this makes upstanding a funny word to use, but I like it, so I'm not going to worry about that.)

I also think the emphasis on small moments of empathy broadens the scope of Doing the Right Thing in a way that makes it more accessible to more people. Marching up to a bully is a tough thing to pull off. Most of us, adults as well as children, avoid this kind of combat because it's nerve wracking, or we're not entirely sure we know the full context, or we don't want to be the next target. I'm all for encouraging self-confident, assertive people to stand up to injustice. And certainly adults intervening among children should play this role directly, whenever that's the helpful move to make. I also think, though, that for kids who want to help other kids, but aren't quite sure how to take on a bully, it's crucial to emphasize the range of effective responses— the many shapes that empathy can take, and the indelible impact it has.

That brings me to the lovely, thoughtful essays in this collection. Many of them are about small moments of compassion and expressions of fellow feeling. Sophie Kleinheksel, 17, writes about learning that a girl in one of her classes was adopted and depressed, and saying, "I can't say that I know how you feel or what exactly you're going through, but just know that I'm always here if you need someone to talk to." That's an example of recognizing one's own limitations, and reaching out anyway. Susan Judd writes of taking her autistic son to a tide pool, and standing with him beside a boy of about 7 with a face disfigured by burns. While other children fled, Susan and her son stayed. "The tide rises and a plume of water covers the fish that we are watching," Susan writes. "My son looks up and moves closer to the boy, who is avidly discussing the attributes of the tide pool. They remain side by side for three more tide intervals. 'Thank you,' I say to the boy. 'You know a lot about fish. Thanks for sharing.'" Sometimes, that's what it's about—just a bit of kindness, of acknowledgement.

I'm also moved by the examples of people who moved across conventional boundaries to play a needed role in someone else's life. When Judy Theune's acquaintance got cancer, Scott, a man close to her, volunteered to help with mowing and leaf raking. He developed a relationship with one of Doug's young daughters, Sally. When Sally needed a date to her Brownie troop's father/daughter dance, Scott was her man. "She was waiting by the door in her sparkly top and flouncy skirt," Judy writes. "There was a corsage.

And, Sally wore perfume." When I speak at schools and community gatherings, I often hear a longing for a stronger web of ties to support children: adults they can count on beyond their parents and teachers. Scott sounds like the best kind of role model for that kind of connection.

Finally, I'm so glad that my book opened the door to expressions of vulnerability and self-scrutiny. This is hard work, especially publicly. But it's so important, both for its own sake and for spurring other people to spread the message. David Theune pulls this off by writing about how painful it was to be taunted for being overweight as a child and wearing JC Penney sweatpants. His mother helped him see that most people have some external flaw that can become an excuse for cruelty and self-hatred. And everyone also has strengths that matter more. As a high school teacher, David writes, "I see people working too hard to fit a mold. And I see others who love their eccentricities. It's always the ones who love themselves who are rewarded with the best friends." It's just a basic truth, worth repeating: You can't control everything about how you're perceived. But you're also not powerless.

One of the best current initiatives related to empathy and character-building is The Making Care Common Project, run by Richard Weissbourd and Stephanie Jones, who teach at the Harvard Graduate School of Education. They recently surveyed 10,000 middle and high school students about which values are most important to them. (The kids came from 33 schools across the country and varied in race and class.) Eighty percent chose high achievement or happiness as their top priority. Only 20 percent picked caring for others. Kids who gave caring low priority tended to score low on a scale for empathy and also were less likely to say they would volunteer in their free time, or help tutor a friend. When kids rank their priorities this way—and think their peers do as well—they're "at greater risk of many forms of harmful behavior, including being cruel, disrespectful, and dishonest," Rick and Stephanie write.

It's possible that the kids in this survey are reflecting the values of the adults around them—even if those adults wouldn't admit to this. In other surveys, the majority of parents and teachers have reported that they rank children's capacity for caring above achievement. Yet four out of five of the teens Making Caring Common surveyed said their parents cared more about achievement or happiness than caring. They saw teachers this way, too.

Rick and Stephanie offer a way to fill the values gap they've identified. They say that kids need to practice caring for other people, and they need role models. They write:

> Children and youth need to learn to zoom in, listening closely and attending to those in their immediate circle, and to zoom out, taking in the big picture and considering multiple perspectives. It is by zooming out and taking multiple perspectives, including the perspectives of those who are too often invisible (such as the new kid in class, someone who doesn't speak their language, or the school

custodian), that young people expand their circle of concern and become able to consider the justice of their communities and society.

Elevate Empathy will help its readers zoom both ways.

—*Emily Bazelon*

PART ONE

Birth of a Book Club

A Conversation Starter

I LOVE MY COMMUNITY. I love it so much that I decided to move back to it to raise my family, to work, to spend the rest of my life.

But it's not without its problems. No community is. And I've always been told—by my parents, my siblings, my ministers, my teachers, and on and on—that if I wanted to work through something, I had to be willing to talk about it.

That's what this book is. It's a conversation starter. By sharing stories of empathy, we are trying to put it in the conversations of your children, your neighbors, your book clubs, or your church communities. Or your yoga studio or your dance classes or your coffee shops or even your classrooms. Really, we want conversations to percolate anywhere people congregate.

By writing about empathy and by talking about empathy, the ultimate goal is simple: we want to ELEVATE EMPATHY.

Important Note: This published book is not for profit. Any profits made from the printed book will be given to a local non-profit in order to elevate empathy.

Personal Reflection

THIS JOURNEY STARTED SIMPLE ENOUGH: it was summer break and I was catching up on some Netflix movies that had been sitting in my queue—just waiting there until I was done with my nine months of grading papers every night. With my busy daytime schedule of coaching daughters in various things, I would watch roughly half a movie each night and then, right around midnight, I'd doze off to pick up the movie the next evening.

But, one night, the movie was so captivating, I couldn't fall asleep. I finished the movie at 1am. Then, I still couldn't get to sleep. What sleep I finally *did* have that night was restless. When I woke up that morning, *Bully*—a 2011 documentary following various bullying stories which spanned race, gender, and socioeconomic status—was still on my mind. I found myself deeply affected by the sadness and by the hurt that not only the students themselves were feeling, but also their families. The film confirmed what I already knew—bullying affected everyone: the victim, the bully, the bystander, the families, the school, the community, and—though this sounds dramatic, I'd argue that it is *not*—the world.

When a book, song—or in this case, film—hits me this hard, my natural instinct is to talk about it with those closest to me.

So, when I visited my wife who was contracted to work at an elementary school two weeks beyond the teachers, I brought the film and its impact on me up to her and to the principal who was also working. An hour later, though it felt as though we had just start-ed the conversation about the state of bullying in our schools, we had to stop talking and get on with the day. But one thing was clear from that important conversa-tion: it turns out that bullying is a topic where everyone has some perspective.

Everyone has played some role: bully, bystander, or victim. Likely, we've played all three parts.

At least that was the case for me. At this point—movie finished and good dialogue with family and friends—I turned to some serious self-reflection. Before I had any inclination of organizing something for the community, I had to look inward. I couldn't, in good conscience, bring up a topic if I hadn't first wrestled with it myself. What had been—what is?—my role in bullying? Like I said, I've played all three parts.

- The Bully

I remember it vividly. In high school, I joined a group of boys in calling a girl "beautiful" in a mocking, sing-song tone. It makes me sick to ad-mit it. This mockery went on long enough to call it bullying (Bazelon reports that the definition of bullying has to satisfy three criteria: verbal/physi-cal abuse, repeated over time, and an imbalance of power). The group of boys (which included me for a short stint) decided it would be hilarious to make fun of someone's appearance and lack of self-con-fidence by throwing a seemingly-innocent (to us, anyway) barb her way every time she passed.

The people who know me best, I think, would quickly come to my defense. They'd make me feel good about myself by reminding me that this kind of behavior was extremely rare for me, that I bullied much less than the average person, that I shouldn't worry about it. But that's the harm, isn't it—excusing our behavior without really understanding the full effects of it? I don't know how much those words, said so long ago, hurt her then—or hurt her now.

• The Victim

I spent a good deal of time in the victim role. Primarily, this happened after my move from Iowa to Michigan in the middle of 3rd grade and it lasted through 8th grade. The target was on my being new and, later, on my weight. I was obese; the target was big. I couldn't identify the feelings then as well as I can now (embarrassment, shame, fear, self-disgust), but I remember many tearful nights. I'm thankful for my mother who sat at my bedside and talked through my days and my feelings and the potential results and the best ways to face the next day.

• The Witness

The bulk of my time as an adolescent was that of a witness. While reading Bazelon's book, I realized that the power of change belongs in the witnesses as 90% of bullying happens when others are around. Yet, as Bazelon writes, "...students...were allergic to snitching: they could see that when kids did report bullying, the situation often worsened for them."

This *must* have been how I felt because I saw bullying daily—repeated mocks and jeers—and said nothing. I suppose it was part of the school culture. I'm sure I excused my inaction by simply noticing how much it was happening and how little others talked to authority figures. The classic defense of "no one else was reporting it, why should I?" *That* is the definition of inaction. Martin Luther King, Jr. poignantly stated, during the battle for Civil Rights, "History will have to record that the greatest tragedy of this period of social transition was not the strident clamor of the bad people, but the appalling silence of the good people." The same is true for the bullying problem. So, the question is this: how do we get adolescents to see this? How do we get them to speak up before they turn thirty-eight?

But, who am I kidding? Thirty-eight-year-old people can use this same advice. If honesty is to win out, I have to acknowledge witnessing bullying as a teacher. I stand by the fact that I report most of it, but I can think of journal entries I've let slide without investigating or handing over to my assistant principal. I've witnessed a hallway pushing which I assumed was mutual joking. But, what's the story I'm *not* passing along? Does that journal entry root in serious depression? Is that pushing an actual dominance struggle and I passed it off as a rare occurrence because I've only seen it once? I must pay better attention to my surroundings.

After two weeks of serious reflection and discussion with those closest to me, I realized that this topic was worthy of more. I *am* an English teacher after all, so I frequently turn to literature to help me understand ideas or concepts. If our community was to have a serious discussion about bullying and empathy, we needed a common language—and a book could give us that. So, it was time to start the search.

Finding the Book

THE BOOK—THE VEHICLE THAT STEERED the community conversation. Finding Emily Bazelon's *Sticks and Stones: Defeating the Culture of Bullying and Rediscovering the Power of Character and Empathy* was the result of some specific questions to those I trusted.

In searching for the right kind of book for this club, I made a plea to my social networks—both face-to-face and digital ones—to tell me what books were leading the way in this kind of work. I wanted to make sure the book was fresh. To me, that meant a bullying book that dealt with both the classic face-to-face bullying and the increasingly popular form of digital bullying—a form that can sometimes hurt worse because the bully is often anonymous. The roads kept leading back to Emily Bazelon.

Her book also had to be readable—not too jumbled with theory for the widespread audience we were hoping to get. It had to challenge us readers, but not derail us. It couldn't be too graphic, but it had to be real. I had high hopes for our first book club.

Bazelon's *Sticks and Stones* was all of it.

Her book uses a non-fiction narrative style to introduce us to three cases spanning race, gender, and socioeconomics. But she does so with a journalist's flair— a flair for facts and research. She makes points, backs them up, and applies them to the teens' stories she uses in the book. Without getting into too many details, she lays out the book by understanding the history, definition, and theory of bullying. Bazelon is quite amazing at pointing out the complexities of the issue—recognizing that there is often more than what we see printed in the papers or shown on television news stations if the case should get that big. She also asks one other critical question, the question we all want answers to: how do we change and get better? In a lecture I attended of Bazelon's, she had a very important slide which shows that, with great care and focus, problems can get better. She referenced drinking and driving and wearing seatbelts. Those problems have improved statistically. Now, as a nation, we're working hard on getting rid of cell phone usage in cars. Bazelon claims that same effort is necessary with bullying and empathy. We *have* to pour resources into improving empathy in our schools and community.

I agree. Thus, the book club.

But, I knew I couldn't do this alone. I needed others on board with the idea.

Connection with Others

AFTER MY PERSONAL REFLECTION AND finding the book, it was time to get moving with more concrete ideas. Through more dialogue with more people, it became clear as day that people just wanted to be heard, that we all had some kind of connection to this topic. I found it only took my casually bringing up the thought of a community conversation before discussions with others was thirty minutes deep in personal stories of witnessing bullies—or of being victimized by them.

The more I talked to others, the more I realized greater dialogue on the topic was necessary. But how? How could we get this crazy idea off the ground? I'm no Oprah. I don't make a book club and have thousands of people join in.

It started with my superintendent. I only wanted to follow through with this idea if the school was behind it. Also, this is a difficult topic and, though my intention was not to bring *blame* to the school, bullying often brings out the worst in people—including direct blame on a school system. Before moving forward, I *needed* to know that the superintendent of our school district was on board. Immediately, he was. I was impressed. Though there was not going to be a lot of money available—which was fine—he did offer to print up some nice posters to hang around town and to provide space on the schools' website as well as access to the district emails in order to send staff and parents information. It was terrific support and it added fuel to the fire.

After that, I knew exactly what to do: have a great conversation with Jill—a wonderfully involved parent of three children in our district and a community mover and shaker. I explained the idea: as many people as possible read a single book over two months with minimal face-to-face meetings and lots of Facebook conversation. Focus on dialogue. She loved it. And she had the idea that really allowed the book club to get off the ground: create a small committee of equally motivated school and community members who would help spread the word.

And that's just what we did. In a two-week span, the small committee met and agreed to speak to any local group possible: the school board, the Rotary Club, the 100 Women Who Care, elementary school parent clubs, our neighbors, families, our email contact lists, and on and on. As a matter of fact, the committee thought it could be powerful to find and advertise some community groups who supported the book club. So, we approached the following groups to see if they were in favor of a community discussion on bullying and empathy and, if they were, we'd be happy to advertise them on our website. The following agreed:

- Spring Lake/Ferrysburg Police Department
- Center for Women in Transition
- Spring Lake Fitness and Aquatic Center
- Grand Haven Tribune
- Tri-Cities Ministries Counseling
- Spring Lake District Library
- Pathways, MI
- International Wellness Partners
- Spring Lake Wesleyan Church

Throughout the book club, these groups were available for encouragement and even allowed their spaces for small group discussions.

Having some significant community support of the book club proved beneficial moving forward. Because of these people and organizations stepping up, the conversation on bullying and empathy had already started—and we had not even started reading the book. We had not even had The Kickoff.

Workings of the Book Club

THE COMMITTEE AND I RECOGNIZED the extremely busy lives we all lead, so, as we were setting up the book club calendar, we wanted to make the "mandatory" face-to-face time limited. We wanted to recognize people's busy schedules while still asking them to think about this important issue. We broke the book club into five distinct parts: The Kickoff, The Digital Chats, The Optional Face-to-Face, The Eat With Eight, and The Launch.

The Kickoff

THE KICKOFF'S PURPOSE WAS IN the name—to claim the official start to this first-ever (in our community, anyway) process of a community book club. I wanted it to be energetic and informative. I wanted to make sure the committee displayed the right mood—one of openness and intimacy—at The Kickoff. I wanted all book club members, before we left, to know what the book club was for and what it was not for.

It was critical to me that this book club was not an outlet for the community to be angry. Instead, this book club was to be an opportunity for real discussion when we were not heated—when parents, students, teachers, and administrators were *not* specifically angry about a certain bullying incident. It's understandable that, when our own children are involved, our anxieties mount, often bringing up anger and frustration, but this book club was not the place for that. This was a place for dialogue and solutions. After stating the book club expectations, we could move on.

Earlier in the summer, one of the committee members and I had the opportunity to interview Emily Bazelon through Google Hangout Live. She, through earlier email correspondence about her book, showed interest in what we were doing in Spring Lake, so I thought it was worth a shot to see if she would accept an online interview. She graciously accepted. She was in constant communication with me throughout the book club—more cheerleader than critic—and I respected her (and still do respect her) for that.

So, we made sure we played some of her video. In the short clip we showed, we used the segment where she defined bullying as it was laid out in the book—and as I mentioned earlier in the reflection. Bullying, as we were using it, required three parts:

1. physical/verbal/emotional abuse
2. repeated over time
3. with an imbalance of power

Having a common definition was important for the community conversation. It's often *very* difficult, especially in the heat of the moment, to differentiate between a fight (an argument or physical altercation where both sides are aggressors) and bullying. Also, this definition excused once-in-a-year shoving. There is anger and it is sad and frustrating and all of those feelings which are not good. But, according to our definition, it is not bullying.

Once we had the definition of bullying, it was time for a sample from a student. A former student, who heard I was leading a community conversation on the topic, shared a piece from her journal that she said I could use in any fashion. During The Kickoff, the student's piece quieted all of us: the other students, the parents, the journalists, and the state representative who wanted to see what was happening with this community conversation.

This student piece reminded all of us that, no matter how small the percentage of students who have a problem with bullying in our school, even one case is a problem. Just one case of bullying will keep that particular student from reaching his/her potential in school and, even more fearfully, possibly life.

"The name calling and judging. They were calling me names because all my friends were boys. They whispered them in my ear in the hallway and class. Girls are mean. Words hurt more than sticks and stones. And those words, those names, still haunt me. I buried myself in baggier clothes, so they did not have an excuse. It didn't matter. I still am those names to them. I still feel violated by them and it's been two years since they stopped. The words still hurt."

Like I said, we do good work in our schools: our elementary schools use Peace Frogs, an organized and trained group of students who help keep the peace at recess; our intermediate and middle schools recently joined Rachel's Challenge, a national move to recognize the good in others; and our high school has an active Be Nice organization whose responsibility it is to spread kindness throughout the school. But, this student's observations still sting. They hurt her and hurt our school. We must constantly work to relieve students of this feeling—no matter how impossible it is to relieve it entirely.

By this point in The Kickoff, we had established the need for the conversation. All that was left to do in the meeting was to communicate the event calendar—including our use of digital social media to have ongoing conversations.

The Digital Chats

WITH THE DIGITAL CHATS, WE wanted to do three things: we wanted to save people time, we wanted to be good models of digital citizenship, and we wanted the voices of many to be heard.

The first purpose is pure practicality. When organizing almost 250 people, it becomes increasingly clear that to get them all together—let alone *half*—is an impossibility. By using Facebook, Twitter, and even an open GoogleDoc, we could rest assured that everyone could be involved. For our particular community, Facebook was the magical medium. Most people in the group had a Facebook profile already, so the organization of the Facebook page was almost second nature. A few adults wanted a medium in case they did not have a Facebook profile, so we linked an open Google Document and included it on the website. This was only mildly used. We also had side conversations going on Twitter, but it wasn't as active. For us, Facebook was the place for us to have meaningful conversation.

But, like Bazelon mentions in her book, our students are well beyond Facebook. As soon as we adults find out about their social media hangouts, they find another one. They are moving on to Twitter, Instagram, SnapChat, ASK FM, and more and more. With all of these outlets for our students to participate, it became increasingly clear that *policing* social media is a battle we adults can't win. So, it was the committee's opinion that if we couldn't *police*, could we at least be *models*? Through our digital conversations—no matter how personal or debated—could we keep civil discourse on the Facebook page? This kind of positive modeling was inherent in the book club itself. Weren't we *already* being positive models of literacy? Just by having posters in local eateries and conversations popping up in parks, we were encouraging reading and talking. Through our use of Facebook conversations, we encouraged civil social media use as well.

Finally, as a teacher, I know that if I hold an open conversation in class for students to raise their hands, only 10% of the class will be apt to do that. Some people are just willing to speak up for the group and others are willing to let that happen. But online dialogue does something else to group conversation; it allows all to be involved. For those who would choose to be quieter or to take their time in forming their thoughts, online conversations are a great way to go. For the timid or shy, it's a place to construct the comment before sharing it with others.

Not everyone did—or could—join us online. For those folks, we strongly encouraged reading the book anyway and even playing a bigger role in our optional face-to-face events.

Optional Face-to-Face Events

WHILE WE WERE PROUD OF what was happening with the Kickoff and the digital conversations, we wanted to provide some moments for optional get togethers with others—strangers, likely—who were reading the same book, who were, in some small way, going through the same process as we. Simple human connection. We wanted to be sure that was a part of the book club, too.

To be clear, none of these events were attended by all book club members—not even close. But I can guarantee that, for those in attendance at each one, it was meaningful.

For these optional face-to-face, I wanted to highlight different places in the community. As we were scheduling them, it was simple to get community partners involved in the hosting. This was a good way to lean on them, to ask for the gift of time and place. Each and every time, the community partner stepped up.

As a committee, we were roughly looking for one event every two weeks. We were lucky to have our first event just sitting there, already set up by our intermediate and middle schools who signed on to the nationally-known program called Rachel's Challenge. One week after The Kickoff, we were able to attend the Rachel's Challenge Community Night where kindness and empathy were the challenge—the challenge for all of us to put out into the world.

Early on in the optional face-to-face events, I wanted to give a viewing of *Bully*, the movie that acted as the spur to this whole idea. We had an open viewing set up at our local library with a conversation to follow. The crowd was small—maybe 10-15 people—but the viewing was emotional and the following conversation was powerful. We had students share their own experiences with bullying and parents who gave their challenging perspective, too. I didn't have answers to the difficult questions they were posing. I never *once* suggested I had the answers for this challenging question: what do I do for my child who is hurting? I only provided the public place for us to come together and ask and wonder and think—and empathize. In my world, knowing that others feel the same way, might just be powerful enough. That's what the movie and conversation gave us—a time to share.

The first Monday of every October is World Day of Bullying Prevention and we, as a group, wanted to take advantage of that. The task is simple: wear a blue shirt. Then, when others see so many with blue shirts, it leads to questions. Those questions lead to discussions. And *that* was the point of the book club in the first place. Though not a meeting in one *singular* place, the face-to-face was happening all throughout the community. A large contingency at our school wore blue, people at our community sponsors wore blue, people in the private sector wore blue. Blue was abounding and it led to some important face-to-face dialogue.

Unique opportunities popped up all over the place throughout this community book club and one was an unexpected offer for a face-to-face event. A local business, International Wellness Partners, which focuses on a holistic approach to health offered a free meditation session. The owner of the business approached me making the claim that inner peace and health leads to interpersonal peace and health. I couldn't agree more. So, we made an unplanned face-to-face event and advertised it via our Facebook page. Again, it had low attendance, but for those who *did* attend, it was a rich experience. We were able to breathe, to be calm in the middle of our hectic lives. The meditation allowed for reflection and breath—and inner peace which leads to outer peace.

We didn't know this when selecting the book, but author Emily Bazelon was scheduled to give a lecture in Grand Rapids, which is only thirty miles from our small town. Unbeknownst to us at the time, Bazelon herself was only going to be minutes away. I've learned over my years that nothing happens if you don't ask for it, so I decided to reach out to her and ask about her travel plans that day. I found, that, if all flights were on schedule and if she was willing, we could squeeze out an hour of her time and bring her to Spring Lake. So, I asked. And she was willing. We were scheduled to have Bazelon join us for a weekday lunch. I had arranged, thanks to our gracious principal, for the students involved in the book club to leave class for the hour-long event. Lots of book club participants made arrangements to have a long lunch as well. This was to be our biggest face-to-face since The Kickoff. But, planes aren't always on time. That's right, the planes were delayed and Bazelon missed the flight. We were stuck—or so it seemed. But, at times, detours can lead to the best journey, can't they? We still all met and split the students up with the adults in attendance. Phenomenal, candid conversation ensued. Adults and students were connecting like they rarely do. No eye rolling. No trying to escape. Just dialogue and it was beautiful. Though we would have loved an hour with Ms. Bazelon, we managed just fine being us, talking.

Eat With Eight

JUST US, TALKING. THAT WAS the idea behind the Eat With Eight event. In the final week of our book club, we wanted to give everyone a voice. We took all book club members and split them into groups of eight.

Let me rewind just a bit. When people were initially signing up for the book club, we had an option where they could sign up, as well, to be an Eat With Eight host. The responsibility of the host was to communicate with their assigned group as to what day during the final week would be best for a get together. Thanks to one dedicated committee member who agreed to organize the hosts, the Eat With Eight hosts were given possible ideas for their gathering. They could meet at people's homes, each sharing dishes to pass. If they were uncomfortable with the idea of strangers in their home, they could meet for dinner out on the town and support the local economy. Or they didn't even have to be fooled by the title of the Eat With Eight at all: they could just meet in the library if that suited the group better.

It was exciting. In that one final week of the book club, we had twenty-five groups all talking about a book on empathy and future plans on how to elevate it in our community. I can't speak to all of the groups' conversations, but mine (a shared Italian dinner with all the fixings attended by a couple individuals, two couples, and a student) involved reflecting on our past experiences with bullying, the student's current issues with bullying, and potential fixes to the problem. We were at table for more than two hours.

The Eat With Eight event reflected everything that the book club was about: small groups talking intimately—and without anger—about bullying and empathy and how we can highlight the good deeds in our community and de-emphasize the bad. Being in the final week, we suggested that each group finish their Eat With Eight discussion by thinking about active solutions to elevate empathy in our community and to be ready to share that at The Launch.

The Launch

WAIT. A LAUNCH? AT THE end? That's right. The Launch came at the end to, in fact, launch us into action. A good teacher friend of mine uses this term at the very end of her teaching hour. It's brilliant. She tells her students that they've learned a lot, but none of it matters if they don't take it with them, if they don't use it to *launch* more learning. That, I suppose, was the idea with calling the final event of the book club The Launch. The committee's vision of the book club was never to have this conversation be the end all, be all. This book club was only to start the conversation, to start the *action* of greater empathy in our community.

So, at our final event, The Launch, where all book club members were invited, we began by reflecting on the book club process, but we quickly moved on to the main purpose of the one-hour meeting: to give physical ideas to strengthen empathy in our community. Great ideas came up: posters in the schools for students to keep their bullying in check, business cards to be handed out at random by book club members to community members letting them know of our mission and to encourage them to join the movement by adding themselves to our Facebook page, a banner hung in a prominent part of the community reminding all that we want more empathy than anger.

Each one of these things happened: we had posters in the school, a book club member donated several hundred business cards with a great saying and directions to the Facebook group, and a banner was made and hung in the middle of our busiest intersection. Efforts were made to elevate empathy in our community. Action was taken from the book club. It was a beautiful effort.

But posters are taken down at the end of the school

year. Business cards—and their funding—run out over time. Banners break down and tear and blow away in strong winds.

There is one thing, though, that can never go away: words. And it's the reason for this book and the following stories. Through the following non-fiction accounts of empathy, we etch a place for dialogue. These words cannot crumble or blow away in the wind. They simply are—for eternity.

We hope these words provide a road map for you to think and act, to elevate empathy wherever you may be reading.

PART TWO

The Community Stories

Open Your Heart

We Are All Works In Progress

EMPATHY—WHEN I THINK OF THIS word, it creates a series of emotions within me. I believe that each experience—the good, the bad and even the ugly—form us into the unique person that we are meant to be. Empathy, to me, is a practice—nothing that we will really ever master. We are perpetual works in progress. Practicing empathy can be scary. We want to say the right thing and sometimes we just don't. Often times, when we are being empathetic, we are in uncharted territory. Being empathetic can be risky—we are opening ourselves up for criticism—we are exposing our own emotions and experiences. But, remember, it is the times when we move out of our comfort zone that we grow the most. Standing up for someone who is being bullied will help the victim—but it also helps you become a compassionate and skilled empathy leader! When I practice empathy, I try to think of ways that my words and actions can bring peace to those who are suffering, safety to those who are scared, and joy to those who are celebrating. We will get better and more comfortable practicing empathy if we practice openly and freely. Learn, listen, feel, practice, love, hug, smile, and never judge. I remind myself that life situations can be hard, raw, scary and intimidating. I also think that, sometimes, the best way for us to be empathetic is to close our mouth and simply open our heart.

—*Holly Johnson*

*   *   *

Strangers

I See Christ

MY WIFE AND I BOTH are pretty busy people (as is most everyone these days). I am an Episcopal priest and she is finishing a graduate degree in Clinical Mental Health while also working part-time at a residential home for adults with various challenges. So, when we do get an opportunity to go away, just the two of us, it is always an immense gift.

This past November was our fifth wedding anniversary. Though previous anniversaries have always involved special trips of some sort, we felt the need to scale back this year, so we did a weekend in Grand Rapids, using some hotel points I had accumulated through my work. We were walking around downtown Grand Rapids, in and out of stores, generally having a lovely afternoon together in the cold, brisk, downtown air.

As we walked, a man was sitting near a tree on the street and he asked me if I could spare a few dollars for a meal.

I think every person struggles with what to do in

these situations. Do you give money if you have it? What if he spends it on something that will only hurt him further? If I give money to everyone, wouldn't I wind up broke? My family pledges a percentage of our income to our church, isn't that how we help the poor?

For me, since I very rarely even have cash on me, our cashless society has sort of become my "out." I can simply say, "I'm so sorry, I don't have any cash or change on me" and then continue walking down the street, feeling slightly guilty until something else inevitably grabs my focus.

I was not raised to give money away, in general, anyway. For some reason it wasn't in the DNA of the religious tradition I grew up in.

Several years ago, when I was a college student pursuing my Bachelor of Science in Biblical Studies, I spent a summer living with a couple in Canton, Michigan. John and Joyce were my host family while I did a ministry internship at a congregation in Dearborn Heights.

One night we were downtown Detroit, getting ready to go to dinner at a restaurant near the new Tiger Stadium. We came out of the parking garage and a woman came up to us on crutches—one of her legs had been amputated. "Can you spare a few dollars?" she asked me, the college student studying Bible.

"No, I'm sorry," I said awkwardly, as I cast a furtive glance away from her and walked on by.

But the couple I was staying with was behind me coming out of the garage. Joyce stopped to talk to the woman, immediately getting out her purse and fishing around to find a few dollars. She clasped them into the woman's hand. The woman said thank you and went on her way. I stood there uncomfortably, watching this take place and waiting for John and Joyce to catch up with me.

Once they did, Joyce said simply, "Jared, you should always give money to people who ask you." She smiled and we went into the restaurant.

She was very kind, almost matter-of-fact about it, but she singed my soul just a bit. She reminded me of something Jesus said, in Matthew 5:42, "Give to everyone who begs from you."

Seems pretty clear and straightforward, unfortunately.

However, that was over ten years ago and in the time in between, I would give less and less. Society (and me) went increasingly cashless. I spent time working in Washington, DC, when I truly was confronted by people in need over and over again. I discovered that walking around in my clericals made me even more of an easy target.

So, eventually, I just kind of stopped. What I do to help the poor through the church must be enough, I rationalized to myself.

But this cold November afternoon, walking down that street in Grand Rapids with my wife, something broke in me. The man asked for money and we ignored him and kept walking down the sidewalk, but only a few paces in, I was struck and could not walk any further.

I turned around and walked back to him, reaching

in my pocket for the $10 bill I knew was there from the change I had made for parking the night before. As I approached him, I smiled and handed him the cash.

"Thank you, sir," he said. "Thank you."

I held onto his hand and looked him in the eyes, deep in the eyes. "No," I said, "Thank you. I want you to know that you stopped me today because you reminded me of Christ. I saw Jesus in you. Thank you for giving me that." I felt a tear well up in my eyes. I brushed it away and rejoined my wife.

"I think I want to start keeping small amounts of cash on me," I said to her.

A story is told about John the Almsgiver, Patriarch of Alexandria, in the early 7th century. Someone applied for alms, but it was discovered by the office that he was applying in deceit, that the person did not actually need the money. The administrative official went to the patriarch and told him. John said, "Give unto him; he may be Our Lord in disguise."

At its base, empathy means feeling the emotions of another; it means not letting yourself be an island, walking through the day ignoring the hurt and fears and pain of those around you. As a Christian, I'm grateful that our Lord gave a method to his weak and sinful followers. If you do not yet have enough of the love of God in you to feel the emotions of another, to love them with action, then do this: try at least to see me in them.

And then, then, the love will follow.

— *Fr. Jared Cramer*

*   *   *

Early on a Sunday Morning

SHE ALWAYS KEPT TWO PHONES on the nightstand when her husband was traveling: the home line and her cell phone. Old habit.

It was after 1 a.m. Sunday and her children had been sleeping for some time.

The cell's ring startled her with an unknown number. Hesitating, she answered.

(Early morning calls never brought good news.)

His voice was difficult to understand, but this was clear: "...needed to talk to someone before I hanged myself..."

An indescribable chill raced through her body; thoughts flooded her mind. Who was this? Where was he? How did he get her cell number? Was he standing in her front yard, next to a tree, holding a rope? Did he know her?

He went on, "No one will talk to me. My family and friends hang up. I can't live anymore...not worth it."

She, too, wanted to hang up. Couldn't. Asked his name. "Jeff." Jeff had randomly dialed her cell phone number. (Of all the luck.)

Still listening, she reached for the home phone— and dialed 911. Muting the cell phone as Jeff rambled, she gave the dispatcher the incoming phone number and conveyed what had happened. Working quickly, the dispatcher determined that Jeff was in—Grand Haven, a neighboring town.

Deep breath—and she unmuted the cell phone. The

next hour was spent with a phone at each ear—talking, listening, and waiting for the five policemen and one dog to find Jeff. (Please, please, please find him—I'm running out of things to say.) Jeff walked away from his apartment for a time, fearing "someone was coming for him," but returned when she requested: "The cell coverage is breaking up…please stay in the apartment, so we can keep talking." He agreed, but asked in a paranoid way if she was speaking to someone else. She said, no, of course not, he had her full attention. In her left ear, the 911 dispatcher said, "Keep him there, or we won't be able to get to him."

Wracking her brain for topics to discuss, she turned to what worked in her day job: asking questions, listening with intention, trying to solve the problem. And Jeff had his share of problems: three DUIs. Lost his job as a lock technician. Divorced parents, fractured family. Twenty years old. Had a GED. Despondent.

Well, at least they had things to talk about. Sometimes life sounded like a sad country song. Jeff was having one of those lives at present.

She told him that sometimes being twenty can be rough, but things eventually look up.

"You know, Jeff, there will always be someone better off, and someone worse off, than you." That phrase was on repeat during their conversation. He agreed, saying, "Yeah, at least I have an apartment. There are homeless people living under bridges in Grand Rapids." He continued, though, "Everything's just all messed up. Not worth living anymore. Just want to die." And so she tried to approach it from a different angle.

On religion and God: Jeff "couldn't get to church." No car. She said, "I hear in that part of Michigan, there are lots of churches. Try to find one you like within walking distance." (Jeff didn't realize less than ten miles separated the two of them and that she knew very well where the churches were.) But he agreed to maybe look for a church, to reach for something that might provide strength to face his issues.

On war: Jeff was torn up about war. She mused that throughout time, there had always been wars—holy wars, and not so holy wars—not that war was right, but that it was reality, given human history. Can't worry about what you can't control. Sometimes you need to have "news fasts" and not get caught up in the world's problems.

On Michigan: "It's horrible here right now, no jobs, I can't find one," Jeff said. "Is it horrible where you are?" She replied that yes, it was—but better times were sure to come.

They always did.

In her left ear, on the home phone, the kind 911 dispatcher kept saying how well she was doing, to keep it up. But she wasn't sure how much longer Jeff would stay on the phone.

Finally, the police found Jeff, who bolted from his apartment—chaos and tasering ensued. She spoke to an officer; Jeff was being taken to the emergency room.

After the police turned off Jeff's phone and she powered down her cell phone, she and the 911 dispatcher spoke about the gift of listening to someone who feels alone and the difference the last hour had hopefully made for Jeff.

In parting, she confided to the dispatcher that her mother had committed suicide many years ago.

Early on a Sunday morning.

Eventually, she stopped shaking.

Then, she slept.

— *Marie-Grace Wayne*

*   *   *

How Do You Cure Foot in Mouth Disease?

I HAVE FOOT IN MOUTH disease. I've had it for quite some time and I can only hope that it's not contagious. What I want to know is, how does one learn to stop putting one's foot in one's mouth?

The first weekend in February, my daughter, Allison, my granddaughter, Izzy, and I went to Chicago for an overnight adventure to see *The Phantom of the Opera*. The relaxing train trip, magnificent opera, delicious restaurants, and fun-filled shopping (especially at the American Girl shop) made an incredibly delightful experience on Friday. I had more fun than I've had in a long time. Allison and Izzy kept me laughing until my abdominal muscles screamed with pain. "Stop or I'm going to split a gut," I cried, bracing my abdomen. Tears from laughter streamed down my cheeks.

Then came Saturday. A day I wish I could do over, like in the Drew Barrymore movie, where she has amnesia and relives one day over and over or *Groundhog Day* with Bill Murray, where he relives Groundhog Day until he gets it right. Only for me, there was no do over, and that day will be one I will always regret.

Allison, Izzy, and I left our hotel by foot to walk the bustling streets of Chicago for shopping. Swarms of people dotted the sidewalks. Our hotel, The James, was located just a couple blocks from the main shopping district. Light snow fell and the frigid cold stung our noses as we paced ourselves with the crowd. As usual, I was bundled up like a polar bear. Less than a block from our hotel, a ragged, legless man in a wheelchair, wearing a flimsy jacket unsuitable for the weather, held a sign, begging for money.

"Look at that poor man," Izzy said. "He doesn't have legs and he needs money for food and clothes. Can we give him some?"

What did I do? What did I say? I said something I will always regret.

After tightening my heavy jacket around my frozen neck, I said, "It's nothing but a racket. These people are bilking money out of compassionate do-gooders."

I had read about the panhandlers in Chicago. The article suggested that people refrain from giving them money because many use it to purchase alcohol or drugs. Welfare and food stamps supply them with funds and, besides, there are a multitude of churches and community organizations that offer food and necessities. Giving them money often, but not always, enables addictions.

Izzy is a child with deep compassion for the less

43

fortunate. She grew a mortified look on her face. "Mamie," (pronounced with a long a—it's the term my grandchildren use instead of Grandma) she said. "You don't even care about these poor people who don't have any legs and don't have any money! You need to say you're sorry!"

Yes, I should have said I was sorry because at Izzy's tender age of 12, she didn't know about con-artists. In her sweet, naive mind, she saw exactly what was before her: a person in need—and she desperately wanted to show tender compassion towards a less fortunate human being. I should have fostered that compassion and empathy. But all I did was burst her bubble and tell her, in effect: develop a hard heart because the world sometimes deceives us and what we see isn't always reality. OUCH!

There are times to teach about reality and there are times to teach empathy.

I had squashed the perfect opportunity to teach empathy as if it were a nasty bug. What Izzy perceived in that fleeting moment was that I had no compassion for someone who couldn't get up and walk. I'm sure she expected me to show loving kindness and to commend her for her own. But I didn't. I failed. And worst of all, I wouldn't apologize for bursting her bubble. Instead, I told her the hard facts about street life and addiction. There would have been a time for that in Izzy's young life, but this wasn't that time.

The fact is, I'm not perfect. I'm not a perfect mother or perfect grandmother. I make mistakes.

There are certain professions in life where mistakes

can have terrible consequences: physicians, nurses, airplane pilots, air traffic controllers, parents, and grandparents, to name a few. What parents and grandparents do and say with our children and grandchildren will mold and shape their lives.

Did I want Izzy to have a hard, uncaring, stonecold heart, or a kind, loving, empathetic heart for people?

If I could have a do-over, like in children's games, I'd praise Izzy for her kindness and give her money to drop in the man's cup. I would have slipped my arm around her shoulder and hugged her because I'm proud to have such a sweet granddaughter. Truth is, I hope she doesn't become jaded by harsh reality.

There are many things that we can do for our young ones, but one very important thing is to grasp opportunities to teach and foster compassion, love, kindness, good deeds, and other noble qualities before they become a lost art.

To Izzy and all children who shower the world with loving kindness—I commend you and I pray you will one day change the world.

"If I speak in the tongues of men and of angels, but have no love, I am only a resounding gong or a clanging cymbal." I Corinthians 13:1, NIV. I don't know about anyone else, but I don't want my lips to be like clanging cymbals to my offspring. I want to close my lips and show my love by actions and deeds.

— *Debbie Gardner Allard*

*   *   *

Things to Think:

- Is there a time you didn't feel/show empathy and later felt it and regretted your actions?
- Have you ever talked with your kids about empathy?
- Is there a particular group of people you struggle to empathize with?
- When confronted by a beggar, how do you respond?

Things to Do:

- Give to a beggar next time you see one.
- Use any opportunity, big or small, to demonstrate what empathy is for your child.
- Donate your time to help a stranger (Soup Kitchen, Food Truck, etc.).
- The next time you see someone who seems to be in distress or might need help, like a flat tire on the side of the road, stop and see if you can help.
- Leave your change in the vending machine and the teenager's tip jar.
- Bring flowers to the hospital. Ask the staff there if they think there's anyone in particular who needs them. Deliver the flowers to him/her (Trust me, I've done this, the person won't think you're creepy).
- Smile at everyone you pass.

SECTION THREE

Culture

What a 9-Year Old Knows About Empathy

I EXPERIENCED ONE OF MY most essential life lessons at the age of nine. Many of you are probably familiar with the television series Home Improvement starring Tim Allen, which reigned over the sitcom world in the 1990's. My dad was a faithful watcher, so gathering around the television for re-runs as a family was a popular after-dinner activity. In 1999, the finale episode aired. I have little recollection of the show itself—just that there was a short sort of moment at the end when the characters finished the final scene, took in what would be their last moments acting as a family on that set, hugged each other, and lined up for a final bow. What I distinctly remember is that the oldest child on the show—Brad (played by 18-year-old Zachery Ty Bryan) was crying, and that I, in a moment of childish ignorance, made fun of him for it. "Boys aren't supposed to cry! What a loser!"—or whatever the 9-year old equivalent for "loser" was at the time. My parents reacted immediately. They sternly explained how it was perfectly reasonable for Zachery to feel upset as he said goodbye to his on-screen family after years of work and togetherness, and that these emotions had nothing to do with gender. Instantly, I felt shame—the first time I remember truly experiencing that uncomfortable emotion. I ran upstairs to cry into my pillow. I felt hurt and guilty, but more importantly, I understood why I felt guilty—that I should have understood this young man's emotions, not mocked or criticized him for feeling sad.

From that moment forward, it was an easy extension from how I should react to this individual person to how I should react to all other persons. In that instant, I learned empathy. While I do believe that, as human beings, we are born with an unusually innate ability to express empathy, I also believe that empathy can (and should) be taught, as it was taught to me this evening of my ninth year. It is vital that we expose our children to these lessons so that future generations are educated in the art of random and non-random acts of benevolence. If I could take only one thing from the world and leave my future children with only the same, it would be the knowledge that kindness—not ambition, greed, or technology—is what makes the world spin. All good things stem from kindness. It is the single entity that keeps us connected to our fellow human beings above all else—and that is what keeps us alive.

Now in my early 20's, what I treasure most are shared moments with strangers: the knowing looks you exchange with someone when a child neither of you know starts screaming in a grocery store or feeling your own heart break when you exchange concerned glances with a stranger crying on a bus or train.

In her book, *A Paradise Built From Hell* (2009), Rebecca Solnit describes fantastic instances of altruism and human communities borne from natural and man-made disasters. Most powerfully, a man recalls standing beneath the Twin Towers on 9/11 and watching in terror as a man jumped from a window above him—"I watched him fall and I remember thinking, How can I help this man? Is there some way I can communicate with him as he is about to die? I don't know...it's what I thought. And for the last fifteen floors he fell I watched and tried to hold his hand, to be somehow in communication with him" (p. 187).

That is empathy. That is the very core of our humanity: feeling so desperately connected to a person you don't know in a time of elation or deep anguish, and wanting to reach out in any way that you can. No other expression could give greater substance to our individual lives or to our collective time on this earth, and that is a lesson worth teaching.

—*Danielle Lucksted*

*   *   *

Worlds Together, And Apart

THE AIR IN CUATOTOLA, MEXICO comes off of the mountains like steam curling from a full cup of coffee. It is unlike the thin mountain air of the Rockies, the kind that makes you pause for another breath. No, the air in the broad mountains of the village of Cuatotola is different, and it even smells different, too. The wind coming from the dark green mountainside smells like warm earth, coffee beans, and, somewhere, a pig roasting over a spit. The view of the cliffs is beneath where I stand on its edge. I pause to drink in the enormous, panoramic scene and remind myself, with awe, that this is the farthest I have been from home. The world suddenly feels so large and my place in it so small. Somewhere the low beat of Latino music breaks the silence. A dog barks. Voices ring out behind and around me—the voices of families waking and beginning again. The stillness of the morning doesn't linger long. I turn around to trudge up the mountain path for breakfast with the cliffs, soaring birds, and curling lips of fog behind me now.

It is the spring of 2010 and I am on what is known as a "Spring Service Project" during my college semester's spring break. I am joined by a group of roughly twenty other college students and two faculty members. Our journey to the near center of Mexico, or Cuautotola, is a laborious one. We travel by speeding plane, dusty van, crowded bus, and veering taxi to reach the first destination of our trip: Puebla, Mexico. I, and others of my group, marvel at this first taste of foreign landscapes, cuisines, and customs. I listen while the more fluent Spanish speakers give instructions to our taxi driver, holding my arms tightly across my chest to brace myself while he steers the car in and out of the lanes on the crowded city streets. Palm trees encircle the college dormitory where we spend our first night. Our first meal is, ironically, our host's version of American burgers and fries. I am grateful for the familiarity, although my palate is eager to try a new set of flavors and spices.

After two days in Puebla, we continue on towards our destination of Cuatotola. The four-hour bus ride is hot and crowded and overwhelmingly smelly and as much as my tired body wants to rest, I can't. We climb and climb the roads, the way becoming steeper and steeper by the minute. One member of our group begins moaning of her nausea. The smell of body odor of more than one person in our group only gets worse, as our nerves are on edge from the steep and curving roads. Finally, finally, our bus reaches what appears to be the village of Cuatotola, Mexico. The village's spot seems precarious to say the very least. It sits, a cluster of cement block houses and teetering storefronts, nestled on the Ajusco Mountains. Surrounded by green, jagged-cut mountainsides, I have the feeling that we are balanced on the very edge of the earth.

Our week in the village is filled with diverse activities. We spend time each day assisting in the construction of a church building. The work involves forming a kind of assembly line where some of our group members carry cement blocks, one or two at a time, over to the other members who put the blocks in the proper place. Four walls and the ceiling of the church are formed this way. Our other work involves digging a cistern for the church and by the end of the job, the hole is nearly six feet deep. Some of our group members hop inside of it and look up at us; they look like children ⌐ down below. In the midst of our sweaty construction work, we play futbol games with kids, lead songs and games in awkward Spanish, and trudge up and down the mountain paths.

I feel proud of our work throughout the week, but I think I feel the proudest when I'm standing alongside all of the people, no longer separated by cultural differences or barriers. We pass bricks to each other to complete the roof of the church building just in time to have breakfast over the fire. Spanish mixes with English as someone breaks out in a song that we all know. I surprise myself by crying, hearing the mix of accents and voices slurring together. The singing is a reminder to me what it means to be human, what it means to share a common heart and bond, though we are literally worlds apart.

When we pack up to leave, it is with a heavy heart that I dust off my clothing before folding it carefully into my too-stuffed suitcase. I do not want to leave the sound of roosters crowing with the sunrise; I do not want to return to a place where I cannot drink fresh tamarindo around the large table with the flowered tablecloth in our host family's living room. We celebrate our week with one last hurrah—a large meal of pork stewed in a thick, pungent sauce for nearly eight hours. The meal is eaten on cheap Styrofoam plates, which somehow seems wrong. I take every bite slowly, ignoring a teammate who is complaining about the 'weird' sauce, trying to remember every taste, every view of the dusty yet lush mountainside. We discard our dishes, and trudge up to the house to load the vans and slowly make our way back to American civilization—

what now seems to be a foreign land.

This trip continues to be formative for me. Not only is it the first time I have ventured outside of the borders of the United States (beyond Canada), but it is one of my life's most vivid cultural experiences. This experience, like most cultural experiences of its nature, continues to give me much more than I ever gave it. What I've been given is the realization that another culture can be just as beautiful, flawed, and intricately detailed as my own. I have been given a set of new eyes through which I look at people who I consider to be different from myself. We share a mutual humanity even if we don't share a language or dietary custom. We always have more in common than we think.

—*Anna Roorda*

*　*　*

My Time in Africa

SEEING A CHILD IN NEED is like having a hole in your chest—and the hole is wide open. You can hardly tend to it and there is not a patch big enough to cover it. How does this relate to a child in need? The child has a hole in his life; the patches are the child's guardians and they aren't capable of fixing it, and I'm the chest. I'm the chest in the scenario because I witness everything, feel it all, only I can't really fix it. When you get the chance to help a child in need, there is no other feeling like it. At the time, it may not feel like you are doing much, but looking back you made a huge difference in the world.

Living in West Africa is no picnic of any sort. One in three people have HIV/AIDS, more than half of the population is hungry, and so many people are left jobless and homeless because of the lack in government assistance. Lastly, school isn't free; so you need money to get somewhere in life.

Malaria to Ghanaians is like the flu to us—only they have no cure. Long story short, I did contract the disease. I lost consciousness a few times; I also lost twenty pounds. And I slept for about two weeks straight. During those two weeks, I was freezing yet covered in sweat and I couldn't walk without falling over. One day when I was laying in bed, tired and out of whack, I heard a knock on my bungalow door.

"Are you kidding?" I say to myself.

I forcefully yank my numb, aching legs off my bed. I hobble down the hallway, grasping onto any windowsill I could reach along the way. As I came to an old blue rickety door, I saw through the screen a local village boy by the name of Kojo. He was 12 years old, about 5'1" and just over 100 lbs.

"What's up, man?" I groaned with my eyes half open.

"Um, hello, can I have some money?" Kojo stuttered while looking at the ground.

"Uh, no, I mean, what for?" I asked.

"Some food, please," he roughly replied in his broken rasta English.

"Kojo man, I'm like dying over here. Luckily I'm

almost recovered but I've had Malaria for the past week!"

"..." He had no idea what I was saying.

"...Sure come in."

Kojo came inside and just aimed right towards a chair in our living room. I was still in the kitchen area where I let in Kojo. While reaching for the bread and jam, I tossed him a bag of water. He knew the drill. He then bit a hole into the bag and began drinking the remedy which would replenish his overworn senses. I drowned the bread with peanut butter and jam to fill the young boy up. I knew that he hadn't eaten in a while so he needed this. By the time I brought the platter to him, all the toppings were falling out of the sides of the white bread. He was very thankful when I gave him the plate. While he was indulging the sandwich I prepared, I laid on the floor and turned on some Chelsea soccer. I was in and out of sleep. I woke up once or twice to Kojo just sitting cross legged on our living room floor. And the next time I woke up, he was gone.

I never really saw Kojo again after that day. In just that moment, I'm glad I helped him out. I wonder if he still remembers the random white man who gave him food because, from my perspective, I'll never forget him.

—*Dakota Olsen*

* * *

Things to Think About:

- Is there a time you felt empathy across a language or cultural barrier?
- Would you be willing to travel to another country or to some other culture?
- What movies have made you think about empathy or change the way you think about an event or group of people?
- What is the culture around empathy in your workplace? Home? Family? What power do you have to change it?
- How do you fit into a culture in which you don't feel immediately comfortable?

Things to Do:

- Instead of letting TV possibly teach the wrong lessons to your children, use the TV as an opportunity to teach them about empathy.
- Create an intentional family movie night where you pick a movie to specifically teach about empathy.
- Reach out to a soup kitchen in your community.
- Find a local group (church or social) who is traveling to a different culture to serve the people and join them on the mission.
- Volunteer for community building efforts like Habitat for Humanity.

In School

The Boy Dancer

STER·E·O·TYPE: A WIDELY HELD BUT fixed and oversimplified image or idea of a particular type of person or thing.

When I was five years old, my mother finally gave into my ceaseless begging and pleading and signed me up for ballet class. The pretty, light pink shoes with the bows on the end, the pale pink tights and the black leotard was an outfit I desired more than any other. Of course, at age five, you don't exactly have the attention span to become a world-class prima ballerina. Instead, you mostly admire yourself in the studio mirrors or stare at your teacher while she tries to get the class to do the choreographed steps. Even though I wasn't doing much "dancing", I loved ballet class. After a year or two of taking ballet classes and listening to all the fun I was having, my younger brother, Sam, began to beg for dance classes.

For most of our elementary careers, we attended a small school called Walden Green Montessori. When I say it was a "small school", I mean we had about 15-

20 kids in each grade. If you had thirty in your class, it was considered gigantic. Walden Green was a very accepting school, always preaching tolerance and the importance of being everyone's friend. Even with Sam being a boy who loved to dance, he had no problem fitting in and making friends. When it came time to switch schools in sixth grade, however, things started to change.

At the studio where my brother and I dance, there is a competitive dance troupe. This troupe is for kids who are serious about dance and travel to dance competitions to compete. These competitions can lead to recognition from dance schools and even to college scholarships. Being in the competitive troupe means spending countless hours in the studio rehearsing and weekends that are taken over by competitions. I entered the competitive troupe in seventh grade and, one year after I joined, so did Sam.

Switching from Walden Green to Spring Lake Intermediate was easy for Sam academically. But being used to a small and accepting school who had students that had grown up with Sam and didn't think twice about him being a dancer was completely opposite from how the kids at his new school perceived him.

"Did you hear about that new kid? Sam? Well, guess what? He's gay!"

"How do you know that?!"

"Dude, he's a dancer. All boy dancers are gay. That's why they wear tights."

I'd like to say that it was because these kids were only in sixth grade that they were so biased and stereotypical towards Sam. I'd like to say that, but sadly, it's not true. When I tell my friends about how my teenage brother dances, or even my friend's parents, I can see the assumption in their eyes and the way they say "Oh, that's nice," that they came to the same conclusion as these sixth grade kids. Sometimes when I tell people that Sam is a dancer, they are even so bold as to say, "So, is he gay?" Whenever this happens I feel like shaking this person so hard until their brain removes every trace of "boy dancer" stereotypes.

"Hey faggot!"

"You're so gay!"

"Dancing faggot gay boy!"

"Homo!"

Being whispered about behind your back is ten times easier than having people tease you relentlessly to your face. Gay. Faggot. Homo. Harsh, cruel words that most people think a sixth grader wouldn't dare to say. Yet, these words were being spewed at Sam on a weekly basis. And it didn't stop the next year—or the year after that. Or even when he got to high school. It wasn't happening as often because kids were starting to accept the fact that he danced. But there were still derogatory words thrown at him.

One night, when he was in eighth grade, I asked my brother if people ever teased him for being a dancer. He said yes, all the time. And so I asked him, "How do you take it? Don't you ever feel like quitting and just having it all go away?"

"Yeah, I felt like quitting. A lot. All the time actually. But why should I? Just because I do something that's different from what other boys my age do, doesn't mean I am gay. Or a homo. Or a fag. I realized that no matter what anyone says, I'm gonna do what I want to do. If I like dancing, and I'm a talented dancer, I'm going to dance."

After having this conversation with Sam, I was unbelievably angry. I was angry about how dumb some kids act and the stupidity of torturing a boy because he loves to dance. While I was at the studio one night waiting for class to start, I had a conversation with the owner of the ballet studio. I told her my fear that Sam was being made fun of at school and I worried that, because of the things kids were saying, he would want to quit dancing. She looked at me and said, "People around here have small minds. They don't like to think about someone doing something that's different from what they might do. Their little minds only think that ballet is for girls and football is for boys. But your brother is a very talented young dancer with incredible potential. If people can't open their eyes and see the doubt that they are creating and the confidence that they are destroying, it's because they're idiots."

My intention in writing this is not to make my brother sound like a friendless loser. It's quite the opposite, actually. Sam has his own friend group and never has he sat alone at lunch. He does well at school and he's an amazing dancer. To me, Sam displays a whole new meaning of bravery. No matter how many times kids bullied and ridiculed him, he stayed with his passion. My purpose for writing this story is to open minds. When someone has a passion, no matter how bizarre, strange, or weird their passion might seem, let them do what they love.

Now, let me ask you this: would you be able to continue doing something you loved, if you were teased mercilessly about it?

Ac·cept·ance: the action or process of being received as adequate or suitable, typically to be admitted into a group.

— *Olivia Kuhn*

*   *   *

Lesson in Empathy

EVERY SEMESTER, MY TENTH GRADE students and I read Elie Wiesel's Holocaust memoir, *Night*. Along with our reading, we also take a look at poetry, news articles, and personal essays from those impacted by the atrocities of war. Our purpose is to understand the complexities of humanity, to understand where our humanity comes from and how it can be lost. And, each semester, we are fortunate enough to have a local Holocaust survivor come into our classroom to speak about his story of surviving not one, but three death camps in Poland. His harrowing personal tale, told with such grace and strength, never fails to move all those who hear it.

A few semesters ago, when survivor Michael Herskovitz came to speak with our class, one of my students asked if he ever felt anger toward the Nazis. Mr. Herskovitz's response moved us to action. He told us that he cannot be angry. Every day is a gift that he treasures, a gift that he will not give over to feeling angry. He freely shares his story in the hopes that history will not be forgotten, in hopes that the voices of those who had their humanity stolen from them will not be quietly lost to history. He wants students to stand up for one another, to empathize with the experiences through which we all struggle.

My students were visibly moved by Mr. Herskovitz's response. The next day as we reflected on his story, my students overwhelmingly felt that they wanted to do more. They wanted to do something to share what they had heard and learned with the rest of our school community. It was not part of a planned lesson. Instead, my students took over our English class and, together, we shared an important lesson on empathy.

The students split themselves into committees. They planned, prepared, and presented an idea to our principal. The students staged a series of "What Would You Do?" scenarios around the school and filmed student reactions. The students wrote the scenes, planned the filming, informed the teaching staff, and filmed three scenes in which students were being bullied in the hallways between classes. We didn't quite know what to expect.

What we learned is that students would step in and speak up. My students interviewed those students who intervened, some breaking down in tears when they were asked what prompted them to speak up. And my students used all the footage to put together a short documentary for our school television station.

The students shared reflections from their reading, from hearing Mr. Herskovitz, from what they learned about our school community, and what it means to be a bystander and what it takes to stand up. At the foundation of all they had learned—empathy. Following the project, some of my students started a school chapter of the Anti-Defamation League and our school has since been designated as a "No Place for Hate" school. And two years after meeting Mr. Herskovitz and reading *Night*, the club and the lessons we learned are still being shared.

— *Jennifer Ward*

*   *   *

Being There for Someone

EMPATHY IS NOT HATRED. IT is not disagreement. And it is not misunderstanding. Empathy is responsiveness, recognition, good vibrations, and community of interest.

A time when I displayed an act of empathy was during my freshman year.

There was this girl in my Women's Health and Fitness class. I did not know her very well, but we have had a few moments where we have connected. One of the times that we've talked together, I learned quite a bit about her; I learned that she was depressed, adopted, and her biggest upset—overweight. I didn't know quite what to say because I can't relate to any of the things that she has on her plate, and that really made me distressed. But what I said to her was, "I can't say that I know how you feel or what exactly you're going through, but just know that I'm always here if you need someone to talk to." I remember a smile lit up her face—even through all her sadness and anxiety. That to me, showed true strength. "It's much better to talk out your feelings instead of keeping them trapped inside where they can do far more harm to you."

After that day talking with her, I can say confidently that it impacted the both of us. I felt better about myself and I think she felt better also, now that she has someone to talk to. Empathy towards others is very important in one's life. It shows you that instead of just feeling sorry for someone you can actually do something about it and take action by talking with them and connecting—and that, to me, is one of the best things you can have with someone: a connection.

— *Sophie Kleinheksel*

*   *   *

Bad Day?

I WAS DRAGGING MY SLIGHTLY broken frame down the brightly lit hallways, sulking from my new confusion in Geometry class. The day was a snowball rolling, filling with unfortunate events and was coming to its terminal velocity. *I just need to get through this day* is what I kept telling myself. As I overthought the single bad grade I received (and considered all the possible worst outcomes of that grade), I heard my name trail from a familiar voice behind me. I twisted and spotted Katie, a fellow classmate in the sea of smelly teenagers. She beamed as she shuffled up to me so we were walking together. Then, as if it was the most obvious fact that everyone knew, she pronounced, "I just thought you should know that you're beautiful." A grin immediately paved itself onto my face. It was so out of nowhere but instantly flushed my sad spirit. She added the cherry on the sundae as she declared, "I just saw you and thought *that girl needs to be told she's beautiful more often.*" I replied with a shy 'thank you' and felt the bitter grey clouds swirling in my mind transform into a glistening gold sun. It was like I was a tub of cold, bitter water and she pinched a tiny drop of warmth into me that spread to every cell in my body. Such a small compliment made my day. It was as if the universe saw the negative energy inside me and used Katie as a puppet to make it positive again. It was stunning to me that she could go out of her way to make sure I was informed that I was beautiful. And to me, *that* was beautiful.

— *Gabby Coates*

* * *

You Choose

MANY THINGS CAN BE SAID about 4th graders, but that they have tact is not one of them. They are old enough to recognize anything that makes someone different but not to the point where they know to handle it politely-which makes them the perfect age for classic, school-yard bullying.

He smells. That is the first observation made about him, and the one that causes physical isolation at the hand of our peers. (It's widely known that if you stand near him the stench just might rub off on you, stay away.) He wears the same two t-shirts, one pair of jeans. (It's suspected they do not get washed in between use-gross.) He plays Yu Gi Oh. (That's an imaginary card game, very juvenile.) He's part of the special reading program AND math program. (You must be really dumb to go to both.) He's a little overweight, with a baby face. (Part of the cause of the smell, perhaps?) His hair is overgrown, resembling more a tangled, dirty, overused mop than the corn silk of everyone else's. (Do you think he's ever brushed it?) His one friend in the class is a girl just like him but a little less smelly. (He's a boy and she's a girl, but they don't like each other apparently. Possibly, he is a girl or alternatively she is a boy; there is no consensus. They're its.) There is a man who comes and talks to only him and sometimes takes him away; the man has an office with the nameplate "Social Worker". (He gets excited to see him because sometimes they go to lunch or something. No one is sure why he gets to miss class, but it's not fair.) He is undeniably weird.

He is weird, and so he is ostracized. If he was sitting in a seat, and now someone else has to sit in it, it must first be scoured with hand sanitizer. The same goes for if he touches someone; no one else can touch the unfortunate individual until he/she has been cleansed. When referring to him in conversation or to his face, "it" is more commonly used than "he". Girls playing jump rope chant the alphabet. Whatever letter they land on is the letter of the first name of their future husband. If it lands on the first letter of his name and someone teasingly says his name, the girl squeals "Nooooo!" Walking in the hall during break someone pretends to be tripped; they stand up and point, "It tripped me!" Everyone's eyes follow her pointing finger and glare at him. He isn't even on the same side of the hallway. MASH is the ultimate decider of the future, and when creating the options, there must always be one option that's bad fortune. Under housing it's the "S" in MASH that stands for shack; under husband it's him. Someone whispers in a girl's ear, "He like likes you". Her eyes widen in horror as she gasps, "Ewwww!" extra-loud so everyone knows she doesn't like him back.

Millions of ways to send the message.

We are not your friends.

We are not your peers.

We are not your classmates.

We are not even your enemies.

We are your superiors.

You are inferior, and you are alone.

Three years before you call it bullying, but just because you didn't know you were a bully doesn't mean you didn't know it was mean. Because a 9-year-old knows that she's not supposed to make someone cry and when she's far from following the Golden Rule.

As the year goes on, you begin to piece together that maybe he's weird for a reason. His grandma was the one that brought him to school. She signs the permission slips; you finally know why it says "parent or guardian" signature. And when everyone went around and said what they wanted for Christmas, he was just excited he was going to get to see his mom. You begin to have a vague notion of what a "Social Worker" is because your mom is a counselor.

It's desk cleaning day and in this particular seating chart, you're stuck next to him. Everyone's desks are open and the room is a chaotic mess of children crumpling papers and throwing away garbage. You've already finished cleaning yours, hand sanitizer and everything, because you never let it get too messy. Most people have finished cleaning by now and those with a little left are rushing. His desk looks like he hasn't even started, overflowing with ripped and rumpled papers. As he lifts a pile of still important, relatively unwrinkled papers it causes a faint odor to waft over to your formerly 99.99% of bacteria dead smelling desk. Good thing your desk is located directly in front of the hand-sanitizer pump. As you begin to stand up to get more, one of your friends starts walking towards you. Wait, no, towards him. Oblivious to his incoming doom, he accidentally drops all his papers on the ground in his hurry. He quickly drops down to his hands and knees, scrambling to collect the papers. Your friend has reached him; she doesn't even bother looking down at him, smirking as she deliberately grinds her feet into his papers with each step, pretending she's just going for the hand sanitizer. Suddenly all the chaos in the room is concentrated around his desk. Every student makes a beeline for the hand sanitizer, each one trampling viciously over the papers. Now they begin to drip hand sanitizer on them on their way back. He is still desperately trying to save the ruined papers, risking his fingers for them. You watch, frozen. He sees his social worker enter the room and his eyes momentarily have a spark of hope. The social worker barks, impatient, "Hurry up! Come on! Grab your papers we need to go!" The spark of hope is extinguished. His frantic gathering has stopped and he simply stares at the mess of papers. You look down at him as his eyes, filling with tears, rise to meet yours.

In almost every definition of "bullying" the term "imbalance of power" is included. As an editor, while reading the diverse stories of empathy that make up this book, I realized most of them share one common theme: an imbalance of power.

He helplessly waits for you to follow in everyone else's footsteps.

When you are in a better or different position than another person and make the choice to use the imbalance of power to help instead of hurt someone—that is empathy.

You don't trample his papers.

— *Carlyn Arteaga*

*   *   *

69

Empathy for Everyone Involved

EVERY YEAR IS A TRANSITIONAL year for kids. I have raised one to adulthood and have two who are teenagers. Their interests and behaviors change as they grow—and their emotions and hormones often lead the way. As parents, I think it is important for us to recognize that all kids are changing, growing and experimenting with who they are. The frontal lobes of their brains are not yet fully developed and the decisions they make are not always based on reason and logic.

It can be difficult to feel empathy for kids when they make poor choices, not fully understanding the consequences of those choices, or even thinking beyond the very moment they are making them. Sadly, some of their choices can have long-term repercussions, both on themselves and others. How we as adults guide them, respond to them and hold them accountable has great impact on how their stories unfold.

When I was in seventh grade, there was a group of eighth grade girls who decided they hated me. I could not figure out why. The only reasons I could think of was they were older. That—and a boy from their grade asked me to be his girlfriend. I had pretty clothes and a new haircut like Farrah Fawcett Majors (a widely popular celebrity at that time). They said I thought I was "all that". In reality, I was a nervous, introverted 13-year-old girl just trying to adjust to this new stage in my life.

Each day, these girls would find ways to torment me. One day, my face would be shoved in my lunch plate. Another day, I was cornered in the bathroom and poked with needles. I was shoved in the hall and called names. I spent a lot of time in the library at lunch time and did not use the bathroom at the school. I was afraid of them and never told any adult until the point when their behavior pushed me over the edge. We were at a school dance and they cornered me, along with a few of their friends, taunting and shoving. One of them pulled my shirt up, revealing my young body to everyone around. In a state of panic, I managed to run from the school to my grandparents' house across the field.

What happened in the next three days ended the bullying.

My dad called the parents of the girl who was one of the leaders. She was pulled from the dance and brought to our home where the problem was discussed between the fathers. Her behavior was addressed—and so was mine. On Monday morning, the school principal called each perpetrator from that Friday dance to the office, one by one. The entire school knew why they were being called. They never bothered me again. One of them moved away for a time and moved back. Upon her return, she made the effort to tell me not to worry— that she had changed and was not going to treat me the way she had before.

By the middle of the following year, a dramatic change had taken place. My new best friend, who would remain my best friend for decades to come, was the younger sister of the girl who had been pulled from the dance and brought to my home by her dad. In the years that followed, we would attend weddings and graduations and baby showers together.

We genuinely cared for each other and our families.

In less than a year, circumstances had changed: she had changed and I had changed. We were kids whose parents and school helped steer us into new ways of thinking and behaving. We learned from our experiences and moved on.

Fast forward to my son's experience with bullying when he came to a new school. Several boys began to taunt him and hurt him physically. Lunch time and recess were particularly hard. His legs were bruised from being kicked under the lunch table where no authority could see what was happening. At recess, physical altercations took place and he fought back. We went to the school to talk to the teacher and principal about the situation and one boy, in particular. The principal literally said the words, "I know him. He would never do that." The problem was—he *did* do it. Our problem was becoming worse because we did not have the support of the school—and we still had a big problem with our son feeling safe and welcome. We took him to a therapist who helped our son figure out some better ways of handling it than hitting back or acting like a bully himself to ward off being a target. The problem got better but still was not resolved. It came to the point where we refused to send our son to school for several days because he was so distraught and we were so concerned for him. We called the parents of the boy whom the principal had said "would never do that" and the boy admitted to doing it. The problem, in his mind, was that our son was beating him in the reading contest where he had previously been the best. He wanted our son to back down and, when that didn't happen, the boy sought to put himself back on top in the way his second grade brain thought best.

To be sure, our son was not above acting badly in his own immaturity. He got into an argument with a boy over a sports team and sent him several inappropriate text messages. The boy's parents came to us and we dealt with our son's behavior.

In the next couple of years, our son became involved with lacrosse and many of the same boys involved in these instances were playing, too. Their brains had changed. Their behaviors had changed. They became very good friends. Those same boys have spent the night at our house and been each other's best teammates.

My story and my son's story both ended well because adults kept their heads and were willing to look at the behaviors of their own children (including us) and try to help the kids learn and grow. All of the kids involved—both victims and perpetrators—went on to learn and grow in healthy ways.

Empathy often goes beyond what we feel for the target; it goes to everyone involved. I believe we need empathy for kids being immature kids, coupled with adults who are willing to listen to all sides. Hold kids accountable, help them learn and give them chances to grow beyond their earlier bad choices. We need empathy for parents of a hurting child. And we need empathy for parents of the child making immature, bad choices. We need empathy for teachers, counselors and authorities trying to sort everything out in a culture that makes objectivity and empathy hard. When we each work from a place of empathy, we have a much better chance of good, healthy outcomes for all.

— *Sharron Carrns*

* * *

Things to Think About:

- Think about the people who were bully/bullied/bystander in your school days.
- What does a perfect school look like?
- What are programs would like to implement into your school?
- What are three things you'd like to change about your school's culture?
- Can people change their empathy levels once out of high school? Have you seen that? How do people change?
- Has there been a teacher who impacted your understanding of empathy/how you treat other people? Do they know they impacted you?

Things to Do:

- Volunteer in your local elementary, middle, or high school: offer to read a book in the library for kids, greet high school students as they enter the school for the day, ask to be a hallway monitor in order to interact with students.
- Next time you have a nice thought about someone, tell them.
- Reach out to someone who looks like they might be having a hard time.
- Stop yourself from engaging in gossip with your peers.
- Try not to make assumptions about students (or teachers) based solely on one of their activities.

- Think about a time someone made your day. Do the same thing for someone else. Pass it on.
- Offer to help someone who looks like they're having trouble understanding something in class.

Family

The Dance

IT'S BEEN DIFFICULT FOR SOME time. Doug was diagnosed with cancer in 2011. He fought a good fight. But, cancer won in the fall of 2013.

It was hard getting the household chores taken care of toward the end. Doug's energy was zapped with his fight to be well. A call went out for help with yard work. Scott responded. In time, the mowing and raking got done. Scott became engaged with Doug's three preschool daughters, especially Sally. Sally liked hanging with Scott, talking with him and wanting to play. Scott pushed the swing, kicked the ball. He shared time drinking lemonade with Sally.

Time came for Sally to go to kindergarten. Scott would visit her classroom. Sally would seek Scott out when he was on the playground or in the hallway. He read the book, *Margaret Flies To The Moon* as Sally's guest reader on Reading Day.

Sally is now in first grade. She attends Mrs. Grayson's Brownie meetings on Tuesday after school. Last Friday, the Girl Scouts sponsored a father/daughter dance. Sally called

Scott and asked if he would be her date to the dance. Scott was honored to be asked.

Scott finished his shift; he hurried home to get cleaned up and pick up Sally by 6:00 p.m. She was waiting by the door in her sparkly top and flouncy skirt. There was a corsage. And, Sally wore perfume.

— *Judy Theune*

*   *   *

Beloved

NOT MANY PEOPLE ARE AS lucky as I am to have two, happily married parents who prove their love for each other on a daily basis. In their marriage vows, they pledged to be partners "for better or for worse, for richer or for poorer, in sickness and in health." That last bit, "in sickness and in health," became a reality from my father to my mother. His care and compassion for her during difficult times allowed me to not only see his true colors, but to see in him what a truly devoted and caring partner is.

My mother, since I was around 10-years old, has had chronic pain riveting throughout her body, causing her to be quite unable to do the things she normally has been able to do. My mother is a strong, brave, courageous woman who sometimes crumbles to pieces when her pain becomes too much. That being said, this change from a mother who did everything for her family to a mother who struggled to do these things was a relatively large change within my family, things that cause many couples and families to split up and leave each other.

As a child, I was constantly worried about this fate. However, I had a wonderful role model, a genuine father who, to this day, loves my mother as much as he did when they first married. My father gave to my mother what not every husband does: a commitment. At her worst, he was by her side, kissing her forehead, telling her how beautiful and strong she was. Even at her best, these words and physical gestures of love did not change. He was there for her, day and night. When my mother would break down in tears from pain, he was right beside her, a gentle hand upon her back and his forehead pressed against hers in a labour of love I have yet to understand myself. It was during these gentle moments that I saw his empathy, his ability to put himself in my mother's shoes and care for her like she was the most delicate flower on the face of the earth.

His empathy and the reciprocated love my mother gives him each and every day remind me that they are not just amazing together, but that their love can triumph every obstacle that comes their way. It is not only a calming, peaceful feeling that I feel within myself that they will never part, but a secure and a loving feeling for both my father and my mother. I am lucky to be a witness to their everlasting love for one another. I am thankful every day that they have each other. My father gives and my mother gives back in a beautifully balanced state of perfect harmony and matrimony.

Their empathy is shared like a lifeline between

them.

— Madeline Leech

* * *

Self-Love from the Husky Section

WE CANNOT LOVE OTHERS UNLESS we love ourselves. But, sometimes, we need help loving ourselves.

Childhood (and adult) obesity does that to a person.

I vividly remember moving from Orange City, Iowa, to Spring Lake, Michigan in 3rd grade and actually being excited for change. My older brothers, both having to make the transition in their high school years, were not nearly as excited. But, even from an early age, I liked change. I liked meeting new people. I figured moving was going to be a good thing.

It was not.

It started with my wardrobe. Due to my size, it was always a bit of a challenge to find a workable wardrobe. Plus, it's not like my parents were fashionistas. They didn't have the money for extravagance. We were a solid middle-class family: Mom stayed home and Dad was a minister. We had money, but not gobs of it. I was ashamed to go to the expensive Husky section of JC Penney where all the clothes cost just a *little* more—you know, for the extra fabric. Besides, I *liked* wearing sweatpants. They were comfortable.

But, the ridicule I felt for wearing those things was

terrible. I remember crying at night over and over. The kids laughed like Fat Albert when I walked by. "Hey, hey, hey" in the harshest tone possible. They giggled when I wore the same sweats two days in a row. They damaged me. I didn't love myself. Until my mom taught me how.

She reminded me that I was smart (I was immediately accepted into the accelerated math class), I was athletic (obese kids do pretty well at Red Rover), and I was kind (I signed up to help her deliver Thanksgiving meals that year). She reminded me that these characteristics could be intimidating to others. She reminded me that these are the qualities that will last a lifetime. A person will always be ribbed for some external look— be it too many zits, too little make-up, too much tan, or too fat. Too white. Too dark. Too freckled. One can only concentrate on self-love. And once one has that, then one can love another.

Now, as a high school teacher, I see that. I see people working too hard to fit a mold. And I see others who love their eccentricities. It's always the ones who love themselves who are rewarded with the best friends.

Sure, I want to lose weight—again—but it's for my health, for my family, for me.

It's about self-love—and the people who remind you of that when you need it most.

— *David Theune*

* * *

81

Things to Think About:

- What's the most important thing your parents have taught you so far?
- What are experiences you've shared with your family and no one else?
- When was a time you were down and someone in your family lifted you up?
- How can you model the empathy that your family has modeled for you to other people?
- Family doesn't have to mean related by blood. Think about some people who have been like family to you. What did they do to get that definition?

Things to Do:

- Thank your parents for something specific they've done for you (a certain life lesson, a time they said just the right thing, etc.).
- Tell your family you love them.
- Be patient when you're family member is going through a hard time.
- If you can tell your sibling, parents, etc. had a rough day, take on one of their daily chores (do the dishes, make dinner, take the dog out, etc.).

People With Disabilities

Baby Bottle for a Doll

AUTISM IS A MYSTERIOUS CONDITION. An affected person is disconnected from our world. When someone is disconnected, it is pretty easy for others to cut corners in regards to greetings, conversations, and goodbyes. Megan was on the receiving end of my shortcuts. I'm entrusted to take care of such children and I regret that this is my cautionary tale.

I love exploring medical mysteries and was excited to read about a theory that explained this disorder. Exact details involved the neurologic inability of an autistic child to empathize. Their brain cells which mirror the actions and moods of others were felt to be defective. The theory seemed to sum it up nicely. Autistic children don't recognize when others are hurt. They don't respond to heartfelt requests. Corners could still be cut for the sake of time and I wouldn't have to expend the effort in making an emotional connection. After all, it would seem patronizing and inappropriate to have a one-sided conversation with a child who was not tuned into my efforts.

Such a viewpoint reminds me of the first time one sees a baby bottle for a doll. It seems full of milk. It is apparent that the fluid level couldn't possibly go down when obviously sealed inside the bottle. Yet, as we all learned, it does. Our assumptions change once we acquire further knowledge. Rare firsthand accounts from a couple of autistic children, Carly Fleischmann and Naoki Higashida , show us that they are profoundly empathetic. They painstakingly type a few sentences over hours to let us in on this mystery. They are concerned about their parents' struggles with a special needs child; they know what makes their siblings happy and what causes them stress.

Expressing their concerns is where things prove difficult. Looking into our eyes causes them to experience a gaze filled with thousands of repetitive snapshots. There is no choice but to avert their eyes. The neural message to extend their hand and make a personal connection gets hijacked and becomes seemingly meaningless movement. Even words are stripped of their meaning on their way out of the mouth.

I now see the simple illusion which I had accepted as truth. It has been taught to me by deceptively abled children. They possess the empathy, that I lacked, yet are unable to show this through a physical conduit. I had the physical ability to show empathy, but it needed to be present to be expressed. Armed with a post bottle-tipping insight, I can now truly care for these patients. Megan and I now connect. Approaching her from off center, giving her a sticker she cannot grasp, and commenting on her beautiful hair are all things that she and I now cherish together. When I gently hug her goodbye, I know that my caring touch is received.

It is now apparent to me that feedback is not needed to

reward our empathy, we just need to get it out there.

— *Michael Warmoth*

*　*　*

Differences Don't Make a Difference

I LEAPED OFF THE SCHOOL bus into the humid air and rushed through the office doors to seek out my best friends, followed by the monotonous click-clacking sound of a girl's cane. The girl is visually impaired—the only visually impaired person in my school. She has a fleck of vision in her right eye, but other than that, no vision at all.

After I found my friends, we idled at my locker, watching the girl drift from group to group of people, occasionally getting to chat about her favorite singer, Lady Gaga, with the left-out kids, but mostly being tuned out and ignored. She doesn't realize it, but almost none of the people are as happy to talk to her as she is to them.

At a distance, we watched her get too close in their personal space and watched them roll their eyes at their friends and turn their backs on her. Little did they know that she was just trying to see who they were, what they looked like, and make friends.

A group of boys were near and, of course, she speed-walked to go talk to them like she does with every person in her friendly way. The way she can always see the good in people before she gets to know who they really are or the way she has the courage to go up to any person and introduce herself makes me admire her. I don't know of any other person who can do that and not be nervous or shy unless among friends.

She walked eagerly over to the boys when one of them made an old squeaky noise that the girl used to do all the time. They still make fun of it. She squeaked back, thinking she'd get a good laugh out of them. Instead, they laughed at her, not with her. The boys in the back squeaked mockingly in her direction. Their laughs sounded like a pack of crazed hyenas.

My friends and I knew it was going too far and decided to step in instead of watching it go on and on. If no one was going to stand up to help her, I would. Clutching our books we stood strongly beside her, as if to say knock it off in an unspoken matter. They knew what they were doing was in no way actually funny or kind at all.

The day raced by and, before I knew it, it was time to go home. The girl packed up her belongings and headed out the doors. Close behind, I stepped out into the bright sunshine, letting it warm my skin, only to look over my shoulder and see her talking to two boys a grade below me. When she departed, I walked past them. Straightaway, he whispered, "What a loser. She was scaring me."

Quicker than the blink of an eye, my head was looking back at them. They turned their cruel minds away as if they never said a thing. How could they be so rude? It bugs me when people ask me if I'm her sister.

But guess what, I am and that is something I am proud to be.

A hero doesn't have to be someone who saved the world or do much of anything important at all. A hero can be a person who is simply kind to others and that is why my sister is: my hero.

— *Emmeline Wachter*

*   *   *

The Tide Pool

IT IS SUMMER, AND IT is hot. The heat rises from the asphalt at the local zoo, assaulting my heels with every step I take.

I turn my sandals toward my son, who is alternately running ahead of me or dawdling behind as we catch glimpses of flamingos, monkeys, otters and bears. The heat has made the animals lethargic and somehow, they seem sad to me.

It is summer, and I am still wearing my son's diagnosis of autism like an ill-fitting coat. Autism. Who knew? The books say that autism affects three significant areas — behavior, communication and social skills. The books say that my son will have difficulty relating to his environment. The books say…

I am lost in thought as I so often am these days, and I fail to realize that my son has stopped in front of the aquarium. His upturned face emerging from babyhood is sweet and earnest. He is smiling and his eyes are alight with a plan.

"Oh," I groan, "Not the tide pool again."

We are headed for the tide pool, a watery paradise enclosed by glass. The smelly little room is crowded with parents and children pressed against one another. The tide rises and falls at regular intervals just like the ocean. This predictable, repetitive movement fascinates my son. We watch.

When my son becomes excited, he flaps his arms. He is excited now and people are staring. I pretend not to see, and I turn to him and quietly point out a fish. A few minutes later, I realize that people are leaving despite the fact that it is almost time for another tide to roll in. I look up and then I quickly avert my gaze.

Standing next to my son is a boy of about 7. His face is burned so badly that it is hard to recognize that it is indeed a face. A little girl beautiful enough to be a Disney princess audibly gasps as her mother leads her to the door.

We are alone with the boy and a woman who I assume is his mother. She is young but world-weary. I can tell that she was once pretty but today she is simply tired. She wears the same expression that I see in the mirror, the silent prayer: "Accept me, accept my son."

I smile at her. The corners of her mouth turn up and her face relaxes just a little bit.

The tide rises and a plume of water covers the fish that we are watching. My son looks up and moves closer to the boy, who is avidly discussing the attributes of the tide pool. They remain side by side for three more tide intervals.

"Thank you," I say to the boy. "You know a lot about fish. Thanks for sharing."

He gives me a shy smile. My son waves to him, lifting his pudgy hand with his fingers turned toward his face. Then the boy and his mother are gone.

I gently tell my son that we should be moving on although I have no clue where we are headed. I find myself speaking instead of encouraging his speech, my words pelting him like the sudden burst of water overwhelming the fish. We have grown accustomed to playing our respective roles of narrator and listener.

I naively thought that as the parent, I am the teacher. I will teach him about friendship, I will show him how to be a friend. I will, I will...

My son has proven me wrong. On this day, my silent child has spoken. He stood beside someone needing a friend.

It is summer, and it is hot. After enjoying a cold drink and watching a few monkeys half-heartedly frolic, we head for home.

— *Susan Judd*

*   *   *

Things to Think About:

- Has there been a time your original assumption about someone was proven wrong after spending some time with them?
- What are the similarities between you and a person who has a disability in your life?
- Do you know someone who has a disability? What abilities does he/she have that you don't?
- Have you ever seen someone who has a disability being teased? What was your reaction?

Things to Do:

- Next time you find out someone has a certain disability, do some research and become informed.
- When you meet someone who has a disability, try to find out more about him/her as a person and not just view him/her as his/her disability.
- Look into volunteer opportunities that would allow you to interact with people who have disabilities.

Be It

See it. Be it.

EMPATHY IS SHOWING LOVE, RIGHT? So it is important to understand there are different languages of love so you can see empathy in all its forms. If you haven't read Gary Chapman's *The 5 Love Languages* yet, you need to. Changed my life. Changed the way I see. Changed the way I give and receive. Expanded the way I'm able to consciously connect to others in my family, my work, my friends, neighbors and community. To people I don't even know. In a nutshell, the five love languages, in my own interpretation, are the following:

> **Quality time** – Time you spend with the other person doing something mutually enjoyable but even more powerful is spending time with the person doing something they would like to do but perhaps not so much you.

> **Words of Affirmation** – Saying something nice to

someone. This could be a simple compliment, either at an obvious or a not-so-obvious time. Showing a person love through language is about saying something when it isn't even necessary or expected. And it shouldn't be exclusively about the way someone looks. It can also be about that person's character or talent. Just say something nice.

Gifts – Giving someone something: either the gift itself is very thoughtful or giving something "just because."

Physical Touch – This language isn't just intimate touch but also the person who loves to gives hugs, may touch your arm when talking to you, or gives that extra quick squeeze to your shoulder as she passes behind you on her way to another place in the room. It can be that extra-long handshake.

Acts of Service – Instead of saying out loud how they feel, this language is about noticing how people show love. These are the people that figuratively "give you the shirt off their back".

I work at a school, so seeing empathy is a daily and, if I'm very aware, hourly event. My career hasn't always been in education. I started out in business, fueled by the desire for money and status. In the end, it wasn't the right fit for me. The hours necessary took me away from my family. Going back to school for another degree wasn't easy, but it was a great investment where the returns kept revealing themselves. They still are. I work in a place where I'm surrounded by the most empathic humans on earth: teachers.

Quality time – The teacher who routinely gives up lunches to just talk with a student who needs a listening ear or takes a group of special education students to dinner and prom when the students wouldn't be able or brave enough to go otherwise.

Words of Affirmation – The teacher rains words meant to confirm and encourage hope in a school: "You can do this." "Your (writing) piece brought tears to my eyes." "May I share your work with other teachers? It's really good and I know they would like to see it." "You should raise your hand more in class. You have the best ideas when we talk in person. The others will have a better experience in here because you can help them learn."

Gifts – The teacher who buys new shoes for a student after noticing the duct tape on the bottom meant to keep out snow. The multiple teachers and secretaries who keep granola bars and snacks in their drawer for the students they know who come to school hungry because they don't have food to eat at home and are too embarrassed to participate in the free and reduced lunch program. The teacher who sends a handwritten note home to a parent, calls a parent, or goes out of his way to see a parent in a crowd to tell her about something good her student has done at school or about an instance when her student has shown character.

Physical Touch – Random pats on the back, teachers shaking each student's hand as he/she enter the classroom, holding on to that C+ paper from an academically struggling student until eyes meet and a smile is communicated before letting go and giving it back..

Acts of Service – Connecting a student who has been in trouble at school but just needs that "break" in order to get launched into the right direction with a real, good-paying job after graduation or taking a first generation student on a college visit on a Saturday or letting a student who has been kicked out of his home by an abusive parent move in.

The beautiful thing that has happened to me is that

every time I witness or hear of an act of empathy it is like a charge to my acts-of-kindness battery, encouraging me to be more empathic myself. I am a product of this idea: See it. Be it. I'm finding the more aware I become of people showing love, the more love I have to give. It is inspiring.

Quality time – The laundry can wait. Put your email away. Call a friend you haven't seen in a while and meet for coffee or ask your mother to go shopping. Turn off the radio. Stop thinking about work. Talk with your spouse or kid in the car. Accompany your spouse on the next mundane grocery-shopping trip. If you have to work or do bills, work on your work in the same room, perhaps at the same table, as your family member doing her homework or work.

Words of Affirmation – Don't just say "thank you" next time. Expand on why you are thankful; "Thanks. I always really appreciate it when you help out without me asking. You're good at that." You can also say "thank you" without saying those words: something like this to a husband or wife, "I'm really proud of the kids. I know that has a lot to do with you." Write a little note or a fitting quote and stick it under the pillow of an unsuspecting family member. Tell a family member you believe in and admire her by encouraging her to take a risk like going back to college, writing a chapter for a community book on empathy, or run for student council. Take the time to offer a compliment to someone at school or at work.

Gifts – Hide a chocolate kiss in someone's pocket. Offer a privilege to a child when they least expect it like staying up past bedtime or paying to take two friends to the movies instead of one. Send a sympathy card to someone who lost a parent—not around the time of the funeral, but on the next Mother's or Father's Day. Let a car exiting out into traffic pull out in front of you so they can get in the lane they need. Always signal the person who arrives at 4-way stop at the same as you to go first.

Physical Touch – Offer your hand to hold to your spouse or significant other while driving in the car. Look the cashier in the eye and fully receive his "Have a nice day." Don't fuss with your wallet or start hastily gathering your purchases. Maintain eye contact, pause to genuinely smile, and say, "Thanks. I hope yours is nice too." Next time you bump into an acquaintance and she reaches to give you a hug, resist the temptation to do the awkward barely-a-brush hug and light hand tap on the back, separating as quick as possible. It can be quick but perhaps give a little squeeze before parting. It can be light but make it last just a bit longer than the word "Hi!" You can tap your hand on the back but make the last tap linger. Make all hugs meaningful.

Acts of Service – Do something you don't normally do to help around the house. Offer to not just plan, but to also make a dinner for a night. Take out all the trash throughout the house on trash pick-up morning. If someone mentions a budding curiosity about something, email them book titles to get from the library or links you know of that they might find interesting. Help a person network to find a job or offer a job shadow. Make a conscious effort to do the thing you always forget to do (such as making sure your phone is charged and with you) because you know it bugs someone—even if you don't think it is that important. Don't leave shoes in piles by the door; make sure your dirty laundry makes it in the laundry basket, or that you don't back over the grass on the way out of the driveway. Be in charge of the collection at work for the next baby shower or bereavement flowers or organize the next Friday potluck or after-work outing.

The more you raise your awareness of how people show love, the more you will see that empathy is all around us: at home, at work, and even during the minutiae of our day, the parts that seem trivial and insignificant. If you see it, you will be it. And the best part is when you "be it", you inspire others to be it too.

Empathy is contagious. Let it grow in you and you will grow from it.

— *Jean Arteaga*

* * *

Resources

HERE, WE PROVIDE ALL YOU need to get started with your own community book club. We encourage you to use our language, use our forms—anything to make it easier for you to get started. Consider it yours. Because the entire project cost less than $1,000, you'll see we used free websites as much as possible. I didn't want to shield that here by getting a new website to host all of these forms because I wanted you to see that this could be done with little budget and lots of persistence.

Websites Used For Book Club

Community Book Club Website—We used the website for all of our initial communication. We linked in videos from Emily Bazelon and a calendar of expected and optional events. We also made sure the sign-up form was front and center in the weeks prior to The Kickoff. http://tinyurl.com/elevateempathysite

Community Book Club Facebook Page—We used Facebook to hold our most meaningful online discussions, stopping once a month for a digital conversation. Since The Launch, people have used the page to post articles about bullying and to carry on the conversation. http://tinyurl.com/elevateempathyfacebook

Community Book Club Presentation—We used this fast and easy presentation when discussing the purpose of the book club to the school board and other community leadership groups.
http://tinyurl.com/elevateempathypresentation

Community Book Club Sign-Up Form—This is the form used in order for us to track the amount of book club participants and to place them into EAT WITH EIGHT groups for the final week of the book club.
http://tinyurl.com/elevateempathysignup

Community Book Club Kickoff—This is the direct link to the full Kickoff at which point the book club was to begin. We recommend The Kickoff to communicate the purpose of reading and to feel a sense of community. We recorded it for those who could not attend.
http://tinyurl.com/elevateempathykickoff

Kevin Honeycutt Interview—Nationally-known education speaker, Kevin Honeycutt, also caught wind of the book club and was willing to discuss with us how he sees the current state of bullying.
http://tinyurl.com/elevateempathyhoneycutt

Emily Bazelon Interview—Hear the complete Google Hangout interview with Emily Bazelon. Because of her willingness to participate in the book club, we all felt more excited to read the book. Emily Bazelon has had a major influence on our community.
http://tinyurl.com/elevateempathybazelon

Other Important Websites

Emily Bazelon's Website—You can buy *Sticks and Stones* here and use all of the resources available to students, parents, and teachers. Bazelon even offers a guide on how to use the book within the classroom.
http://emilybazelon.com/

The Bully Project—This website will inform you about the documentary film, *Bully*, and all of the continued steps the filmmakers have made to reduce bullying in our schools.
http://www.thebullyproject.com/

Shane Koyczan's Website—Shane is a spoken word artist whose poem "To This Day" is essential viewing for anyone working through bullying. We viewed the poem in The Kickoff.
http://www.shanekoyczan.com/

Rachel's Challenge—Our intermediate and middle schools are official Rachel's Challenge schools. Rachel's

Challenge is about creating safe school environments so all students can flourish.
http://www.rachelschallenge.org/

Stomp Out Bullying—Here you can learn about how to be an activist as well as more specific information about Blue Shirt Day if you and your organization would like to join the movement.
http://www.stompoutbullying.org/

Sponsor Websites

Spring Lake Schools—Without the school's support, this project would never have left the ground. It takes a strong school to be ready and willing to have this conversation.
http://www.springlakeschools.org/

Spring Lake District Library—Our local library encourages literacy of all kinds. They supported the book club by advertising the club and by keeping a couple of books always in stock for those who wanted to read, but couldn't afford, the book.
http://sllib.org/

Spring Lake Fitness and Aquatic Center—This health facility recognizes the health of the whole person and was willing to host an event.
http://www.slcfac.com/

Center for Women in Transition—This organization works to make our communities safer for women and children suffering domestic and sexual violence.
http://www.cwitmi.org/

Grand Haven Tribune—The local newspaper provides information to the public and was instrumental in sharing book club details along the way.
http://www.grandhaventribune.com/

Tri-Cities Ministries Counseling—This organization offers counseling services to anyone in our tri-cities area regardless of financial situation.
http://www.tcmcounseling.org/

Pathways, MI—This organization dedicates its services to helping children, adults, and families make positive changes in their lives.
http://www.pathwaysmi.org/

International Wellness Partners—This local company dedicates its efforts to supporting, teaching, and inspiring individuals to healthy bodies and minds.
http://www.lisawlee.com/

All Shores Wesleyan Church—This local church provides much support to the community. In their own words, the church wants people to know them by their love.
http://www.allshores.org/

Have specific questions? Contact me directly.
Email: davidtheune@gmail.com
Twitter: @DavidTheune

Visit our website: www.ElevateEmpathy.com

Made in the USA
Middletown, DE
21 October 2014